# 67 lyrics 4 u

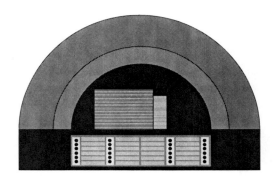

Maxime Alix Gilles

*AuthorHouse™*
*1663 Liberty Drive, Suite 200*
*Bloomington, IN 47403*
*www.authorhouse.com*
*Phone: 1-800-839-8640*

*© 2008 Maxime Alix Gilles. All rights reserved.*

*No part of this book may be reproduced, stored in a retrieval system, or transmitted by any means without the written permission of the author.*

*First published by AuthorHouse 2/5/2008*

*ISBN: 978-1-4343-5014-5 (sc)*

*Printed in the United States of America*
*Bloomington, Indiana*

*This book is printed on acid-free paper.*

# dedication

To the many people who share their most personal moments, intimate thoughts, last breaths of life and human triumph with me on a daily basis. This book is my quest to acknowledge how profoundly you influence my perspective and appreciation of life.

A special thanks to the brilliant, constructive criticisms of Shirley Squires, Robin Roberts and Doris Gilles, for editing "67 lyrics 4 u".

I extend a special blessing as well as many years of joy to Robin, Shirley and their long awaited daughter, Melanie .

# contents

forward .................................................................. xi
**hooked** ............................................................... **1**
   just lookin ......................................................... 3
   flirt ..................................................................... 5
   strokin ................................................................ 7
   big woman love ................................................ 9
   summit ............................................................. 11
   fire love ............................................................ 13
   affair ................................................................. 15
   ever wonder .................................................... 17
   fumbled ........................................................... 19
   gemini girl ...................................................... 21
   her name is .................................................... 24
   infatuation ...................................................... 26
   just fabulous .................................................. 28
   dance with u .................................................. 30
   late .................................................................... 32
   sexy hot ........................................................... 34
   silhouettes ...................................................... 36
   back it up ....................................................... 38
   sweat ................................................................ 40
   contagious ...................................................... 42
   my apple ......................................................... 44
   breathtaking ................................................... 46
   daydream ........................................................ 48
   my Cuba girl ................................................. 50
   reasons for love ............................................. 52
   sunshine .......................................................... 54
   wish .................................................................. 56
   you got it ......................................................... 58
   angel eyes ....................................................... 60
**diversion** ...................................................... **67**
   your butt ......................................................... 69

## inspired .................................................................. **71**
    you gotta give ........................................................... 73
    just be true ............................................................... 75
    crazy dreams ............................................................. 77
    just luck ................................................................... 79
    laugh ....................................................................... 81
    shake it off ............................................................... 83
    ask ........................................................................... 85
    let "you" be .............................................................. 87
    live my dreams ......................................................... 89
    suspended ................................................................ 91
    water ....................................................................... 93

## diversion ................................................................ **95**
    the designer ............................................................. 97

**turbulence** ............................................................................**99**
    missing you ..................................................................101
    did i turn you off? .......................................................103
    forgive me girl .............................................................105
    don't try .......................................................................107
    got a fake life .............................................................109
    separate lives ..............................................................111
    so be ..............................................................................113
    restless ..........................................................................115
    suspicions ....................................................................117
    gotta go ........................................................................119
    over you .......................................................................121
    goodbye my love ........................................................123
**diversion** .............................................................................**125**
    sticky wicky ................................................................127

**perspective** ............................................................. **129**
    troubled ..................................................................131
    gotta move on .......................................................133
    butterfly rage .........................................................135
    paycheck .................................................................137
    my 911......................................................................139
    patriot ......................................................................141
    tin shed ...................................................................143
    look for love ..........................................................145
    forgive .....................................................................148
    perspective.............................................................150
**diversion** ................................................................. **153**
    Vegas girl................................................................155

# forward

"67 lyrics 4 U" is a collection of human experiences inspired from my own life and the stories shared by patients, friends and family.

The lyrics represent my personal journey and serve as a vehicle for others to contemplate significant events in their own lives.

The pieces herein are organized thematically into four sections: the first represents the energy and hope of a budding romance, the second part communicates messages of inspiration from diverse life events, section three focuses on facets of love relationships coming to an end. In the last section I share a series of perspectives that enables me to achieve peace and acceptance in my own life.

Each piece in this collection is written in the form of a lyric and therefore a more melodic expression of my personal journey.

Open your mind and soul to the messages implicit in these works. Many if not all will resonate with you and hopefully deepen your own appreciation for who and what you are.

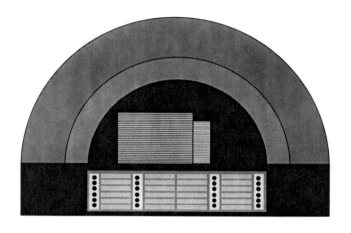

# hooked

# just lookin

**verse**

bustin out the salon
you caught my eye
at attention

on my way for coffee
when you walked by
your eyes caught me

staring at you
just excites me
i want those lips workin on me

got me switchin
running errands
follow you forbidden

looks like
you' re alone
i know you gotta dig my bones

got in two steps
to work you
forgot your man
was right behind you

**refrain**

didn't want you
anyway

just lookin
i'm on my way

didn't want to
block your man

it's code
you gotta
understand

# flirt

### verse

love locked eyes
from across the room
got tunnel vision
can i run to you

see you movin
groovin all the moves
all angles perfect
can i make love to you?

you haven't spoken
i don't need words
for now i'm dreamin
bodies lock in flirt

time to go
your place or mine
the club is closed
but i got more time

sunrise here
got u in my bed
guess i'll miss work
let's make love instead

**refrain**

let's flirt
grab a bottle

i'll pour the wine
lick my lips

i'll caress your shrine
time suspended

i got all night
take your clothes off
let's do this right

# strokin

**verse**

cruzin to be movin
letting time just a wastin
i got nobody home
and there is nowhere to go

i'll give you a ride
cuz i'm looking so fly
where you gotta go
get ya there in no time

cuz i'm feelin my ride
and i want you inside
where i'll make you go
you'll be strokin for more

cruzin and feelin
like the king of my jungle
once you arrive
you'll be sexed and humble

don't try to leave
cuz i strike like a snake
my venom so potent
your wet dreams while awake

**refrain**

cuz i'm strokin and cruzin
i'm lookin so hot
got people staring
at my rims and my block

cuz i'm strokin and cruzin
looking for you
come play with me inside
and i'll show you my ride

# big woman love

**verse**

she's no size two
but she'll rock with you
she'll love you so
make ya never let go

when she gives you love
you just feel it so
she'll squeeze u hard
like a python's blow

she's a plus now
in every way
she'll eat your heart out
just like they say

she's a sweetheart
and she got sugar to sin
you're never lonely
she's happy in her skin

she'll pamper you
make you close your eyes
she'll rock your world
with her thunder thighs

she'll adore you
cuz you her man
don't you worry
Halle Berry understands

continued ...

treat her good
cuz it's all in the heart
love her right
and she'll keep you hard

when you old
it don't matter none
wrinkles sag
but your soul stays fun

keep her well
you got a lot to please
make her smile
you got her on her knees

**refrain**

she's your woman
all woman
big woman
love woman

she'll love you
out of your mind
that's why the skinny
guy's right behind

she's your woman
treat her right
keep her smiling
right through the night

# summit

**verse**

can i ride your elevator
can i take you to the top
can i take you to my summit
where we will never stop

can i let you see above me
can i make you smile again
can i show you what you've been through
and you'll be much stronger then

can you see that life is awesome
can you feel it's meant to live
can you sense that nothing's easy
where you've got to learn to give

can you have some peace inside you
can you come to terms with life
can you let the faith inside you
win the daily war outright

**refrain**

you've got to believe
you've got to fall back
you've got to let go
it's as simple as that

you've got to have faith
you've got to walk tall
you've got to just know
that you'll have it all

# fire love

**verse**

surround me with
purple
violet
a beautiful red
a mantle's reflection
fire kisses instead

soothed
tranquil
your figure lays still
state of mind
erotic dreams
of your journey with me

your image
created
erotic thoughts now divine
this passion
exists beyond
the limits of time

can i caress
your body
your mind and soul
love just imagine
don't ever let go

eyes closed
never wake
this dream just can't end
please never wake me
this can't be pretend

**refrain**

can i steal your kiss
in the fire of love
can i live a dream
i can't get enough

can i just pretend
that our fire still burns
can i have your hand
like it's always my turn

can i love you hard
like it's my last day
can i let you know
there's no other way

i love you so much
i burn deep inside
this fire of love
has me mesmerized

# affair

**verse**

i remember the time
when i first passed you by
your cleavage was flirting
my eyes just said hi

i remember that walk
like a cat on the prowl
your hips needed taming
the city block howled

i'm not sure what drew me
was it fate or my envy
your soul breathed the life
that was missing inside me

i knew i was married
but i didn't even care
for some obvious reason
the connection was there

i remember your eyes
they mirrored my soul
it tore me to pieces
when i had to let go

my marriage was failing
well before you came true
you kept me smiling
through the times that were blue

continued ...

i'm sure you've moved on now
i myself i'm alone
i'm thankful i met you
i'm free and moved on

you taught me to live
every moment in heat
to dream with passion
to love without sleep


**refrain**

cuz i have no reason
to be afraid
no reason to live in shame

cuz i have no regrets
making love to you
no regrets about this rendezvous

# ever wonder

**verse**

every time i see you
i don't know what to do
you have me feelin lonely
since i know i can't have you

what's your situation
the state of your affairs
your every moonlight kiss
like the sun always there

i text to feel your voice
cramped fingers asleep they fall
i dream of this connection
maybe one day have it all

so beautiful your being
many years a vintage wine
i wonder through the storm
if you're my sunshine after time

**refrain**

don't you ever wonder
why two paths now cross

don't you ever wonder
why the time was lost

yes i always wonder
how it feels to have you close

yes i always wonder
if it's me you think of most

# fumbled

**verse**

fumbling words around you
standing nervous
weak at the knees

defined moments ago
at a distance
my heart intrigued

so long i hope to tell you
that one day
you'll be mine

you may not feel the same
but in my heart
it's already time

tomorrow
is never promised
i live for everyday

so now you know
i like you
in just this special way

**refrain**

u got me fumbling
standing weak at the knees
can't get my words out
to express what i mean

u got me fumbling
standing weak at the knees
can't believe i love u
that's just how i feel

# gemini girl

**verse**

we've been talking a while
texting like mad
calling you more
starts making me sad

i saw you last night
i know it's been long
lip gloss and sexy
a ring told me wrong

i can't help but feel
the way that i do
you crazy and funny
i wanna see you

you look so damn good
you tortured me so
your body so perfect
in a radiant glow

having a drink
or dinner for two
girl it didn't matter
i just wanna see you

i wish you were two
my Gemini girl
i wouldn't have to share
and show you my world

continued ...

for now i will dream
and know it's the end
cuz i can't have you
unless it's pretend

although you called me
to just reconnect
destiny calls
i have no regrets

i guess our paths cross
a mystery still
it's like when i see you
my heart just stands still

life is so funny
it doesn't make sense
but what's meant to be
is true in the end

**refrain**

my Gemini girl
got me crazy for you
Gemini
Gemini
got me thinking of you

my Gemini girl
i just wanna hold you
closer
closer
want to feel your truth

my Gemini girl
got me in a bind
losing
losing
got me losing my mind

my Gemini girl
couldn't sleep last night
Gemini
Gemini
one day it will be right

# her name is

**verse**

if you talk to her you'll know
she's contagious
it's in her soul

if you need her she's your friend
she's so honest
don't pretend

if you follow her you'll see
she's unselfish
as can be

if she loves you just watch out
she'll spoil u crazy
ain't no doubt

if you cross her
she'll be fair
it's her ideology

if you pass her don't forget
so damn stunning
she'll make you sweat

if you share your heart
she'll take it
done without regret

**refrain**

so sweet
so beautiful
so true
her spirit breathes life
inside of you

it's her ideology
its simplicity
it's the way that
life was meant to be

# infatuation

**verse**

i wonder who you are
i see you everyday
your smell turns me on
when you walk my way

don't know your name
no stranger to my mind
my mind's undressed you
so many many times

sexy so gentle
you stand without flaw
soft spoken so confident
i'm captured in awe

can you be this perfect
i imagine it true
damn you so hot
can't get my mind off of you

## refrain

infatuated
with your every move

infatuated
i am lost in you

infatuated
come sleep with me

infatuated
be my ecstasy

# just fabulous

**verse**

you look
fabulous in that dress
when you walk in the room
the men are a mess

you look
sensational to me too
are u here alone?
cuz i've fallen for you

you look
magical to us all
the way you walk
so graceful and tall

you look
beautiful with those eyes
can i stare at you?
they just mesmerize

you are
contagious with that smile
can i talk with you?
cuz i can't wait one while

you are
a walkin' dream coming true
come closer to me
i'm in love with you

**refrain**

fabulous
so fabulous
girl only you can wear that dress

fabulous
so fabulous
girl my heart's a mess

fabulous
so fabulous
girl i must confess

fabulous
so fabulous
girl you're just the best

# dance with u

**verse**

feel the beat
sweep your feet
let the rhythm
give ya body heat

feel the words
shout them out
let the feelings
bust it out

feel your partner
touch their pores
let them know
you want some more

feel the sweat
kiss your brow
move your hips
so sexy now

feel the night
see the moon
brush the breeze
just be the groove

**refrain**

i dance all night
  feelin right

i dance all night
  until daylight

i dance all night
i'm feeling crude

i dance all night
my mood is you

# late

**verse**

late brandy
candlelit room
ice cubes melting
retro tunes

dream ecstasy
long overdue
sense the feeling
my heart racing for you

passion crave
infatuation clone
romance me
just freak my bones

leave me hungry
quarter past four
bedsheets missing
i want some more

**refrain**

crack my ice
let's roll some dice
let me touch you
it'll be real nice

don't you worry
about a thing
let me hold you
this ain't no fling

# sexy hot

**verse**

i want you here with me
can't wait for you no more
you got me feeling hot
come on walk through that door

i hear your voice and say
it makes me wanna play
come crawl inside of me
let's go all the way

i climax everyday
the very thought of you
my body's hot to play
i'm making love to you

i want to scream your name
let it echo everyday
i wanna cum with you
let's just freak all day

**refrain**

you
so sexy hot
you make me wanna move
in ways
i never thought

you
so sexy hot
you know you got that walk
makes me horny
don't wanna just talk

# silhouettes

**verse**

silhouettes in the dark
motions at random
taste your sweat
let us fathom

whisper something
make your move
passions grinding
passions soothed

shadows dance
as one heart knows
sweat in fire
take off your clothes

intense desire
now motions thrill
only breathe
my pulse now still

sunrise comes
the morning dew
wet kisses come
how i love you

**refrain**

be my shadow
never leave
be my shadow
just receive

i love you more than words can say
i love you more than yesterday

# back it up

**verse**

turn around
let me see your dress
lock the door
cuz i must confess

back it up
want to give you me
get undressed
skin is all we need

let me touch
feel your tender curves
let me grind
stimulate your nerves

back it up
scream you ain't got sense
wrap your legs
and lets get intense

don't wake now
rest your body some
i'll be back
like the morning sun

back it up
i want some more
more of you
come through that door

**refrain**

back it up
i'm a player

back it up
i can't love

back it up
just remember

i'm satisfied
when you've had enough

so just back it up
back it up to me

# sweat

**verse**

sweat the windows
blankets of steam
lost in kisses
slippery bodies team

let darkness mystify
a sexual moment
glistening angles
breath sounds potent

experience a climax
horizons of your mind
my sexual universe
come back anytime

live my dream
a passionate curse
such moments erotic
let me let you come first

a moment erotic
the moon only sees
bedsheets uncovered
just lay next to me

call me tomorrow
if you wanna play
my schedule's clear
you know i got all day

**refrain**

sweat
build the tension
nice and slow

sweat
feel the passion
let it all go

sweat
scream my name
let the neighbors know

sweat
i'm the man
and i'll give ya more

# contagious

**verse**

since a mutual introduction
we text our every say
since i really got to know ya
your words just make my day

although i never saw you
your voice was just so sweet
although i never held you
you triggered my wet dreams

things started out with promise
just started feeling good
now i got the picture
i feel misunderstood

i never meant to touch you
in ways i now regret
i never realized
my hands were just so wet

you're just so contagious
i caught you by surprise
now it's a situation
did u feel compromized?

i hope you can forgive me
let's start to talk again
let's build that bond together
should've started out as friends

## refrain

so contagious
this you gotta know
i wanna look at you
i wanna to let it flow

so contagious
can't just be friends
i wanna be with you
i want to over again

so contagious
don't close the door
i wanna touch you now
i want some more

# my apple

**verse**

can i take a bite out of your apple
cuz you look so sweet to me
can i steal that kiss you promised
i'll love you fearlessly

can i stare at you and wonder
cause i can't believe your real
can i wrap you in my arms
you've got such sex appeal

can i bring you in my life
cause i love the who in you
can i dream of this forever
in my secret rendezvous

can you tell me that you love me
erotic whispers in my ear
you're the apple of my eye
this i know without a fear

**refrain**

you make me happy everyday
be my apple you're so sweet
i want to taste you in every way
get between me and my sheets

you make me love myself again
be my moment that won't end
i want to share all time with you
as more than just your friend

# breathtaking

**verse**

i never need your picture
only the whisper of your voice
destiny has us together
just by divine choice

i never knew conversations
could begin without end
it's so beautiful to know
i now have a best friend

i never thought that i'd be sad
if i missed you for a day
such a feeling just confirms
i'm in love in every way

i never thought my mind
could underestimate your looks
the picture that you sent me
confirms that i am hooked

## refrain

you're breathtaking
captivating in every way

you're breathtaking
makes me want you everyday

you're breathtaking
i wish i could hold you now

you're breathtaking
i'm in love again somehow

you're breathtaking
simply beautiful

you're breathtaking
i love you so

# daydream

**verse**

come to me
whisper in my ear
bite my lip
love me
without fear

leave me wishing
that you
never left
i keep on dreaming
my mind won't rest

it's you i think of
caught in a trance
all i think of
is this romance

work just seems
to last all day long
at home with you
is where i belong

you got me holding
your body
and mine
crazy love
ahead of my time

it's you i dream of
with passion
no fear
the smile on my face
won't disappear

## refrain

i'm caught in a daydream
so real
so true
the color of love
so blessed to have you

i'm caught in your web
so i won't fight to leave
so simple to see
it is you that i need

caught in a daydream
that lasts all night long
the sun and the moon
have all heard my song

# my Cuba girl

**verse**

you're my Cuba
you're my sexy girl
you look so good
you mixed out of this world

you're the cream
in my coffee
you're the sugar
in my cone

you're the whip cream
on my sundae
you're the life
in my soul

you drive me crazy
with the way you talk
you got me melting
the way you dress and walk

you dance like magic
you love without fear
you make my troubles
all disappear

you my Cuban girl
my forbidden fruit
you my lovely lady
i'm in love with you

continued ...

u my Remy Martin
my VSOP
meet at the lounge
my Cuba got me

let's share this cigar
celebrate our time
we sexy together
we so damn fine


**refrain**

Cuba
Cuban
VSOP
i see the girl that was meant for me

Cuba
Cuban
VSOP
i'm feelin you girl inside of me

# reasons for love

**verse**

sitting one day
i was thinking
of the reasons why you make me smile

then i realized
i couldn't keep track
of these happy love miles

reason number one
i knew you were the one

reason number two
didn't take long to fall for you

reason number three
girl your vibe is me

reason number four
you leave me always wanting more

reason number five
you're the reason i'm alive

reason number six
you're just never in my mix

reason number seven
simple you're my heaven

reason number eight
that our love is no mistake

continued ...

reason number nine
is that your sixty nine is fine

and reason number ten
is that this list just has no end

So Matthew 7:7
gave me you to truly love
cuz truly in my mind
the reasons are never just enough


**refrain**

so many reasons
that i love you

so many reasons
that you make me smile

so many reasons
that i need you

so many reasons
why you're worth my while

# sunshine

**verse**

as you lay beside me
so sound asleep
i see the morning sunlight
caress your chiseled cheeks

all i do is stare
and imagine a time
when despite the odds
you would one day be mine

your beauty lays rooted
from deep within
even the morning sun
embraces your perfect skin

breathe your soul
a sweetness untouched
you're incredible
can't hold you enough

in peace you lay silent
beauty holds time still
i want such moments
from yesterday until

the rose i leave you
is symbolic of course
of how my love my passion
crave you in full force

**refrain**

sunshine
you made me smile again

sunshine
i will love you to the end

sunshine
i wish you loved me too

sunshine
you know i'll always miss you

# wish

**verse**

i see the sun the stars
my moon reflected in your eyes
i realize you're the reason
i feel so alive

i waited so very long
to meet someone like you
just like a dream
you wish someday comes true

i wish that the day
so soon will come
when you realize
it's you i worship under my sun

i want to let you know
just in case i forget
the joy you bring to me
i have no regrets

**refrain**

i wish to have you
dance on my floor

i wish that i could
see you some more

i wish that life
would let us be free

to share but a moment
in our eternity

# you got it

**verse**

not playing games
no more
lights on
come through that door
let me see your face
the eyes
that keep me mesmerized

with you
i'll build my life
you got it
be my wife
let me show you
happy times
will you be
my vintage wine

if this is what you want
don't put up that weak front
i knew with what we had
without you i'd be sad

girl you understand
what really makes a man
without you there's no way
i could ever even stand

that's just because
you see
you get what others miss
you got it girl you see
you got it just like this

continued …

that's just because
you're true
you get what life's about
you got it
girl you see
i'm so happy
i can shout


**refrain**

did u get it
cuz i got it

did you feel it
cuz i want it

did you see it
cuz i have it

got it baby
just for you

did u get it
cuz i got it

did you feel it
cuz i want it

did you see it
cuz i have it

got it baby
you so true

# angel eyes

**verse / duet**

(he)

i see your picture
i can't believe
are you really that crazy for me?

so beautiful
your smile takes away
the pain inside of me

(she)

i can't believe
my dreams have come true
who knew but only me

open your heart
allow something new
you're the man for me

continued ...

(he)

you're so perfect
i can't believe
are you my angel in disguise?

i feel our vibe
we truly connect
it's mirrored in your eyes

(she)

i'm crazy for you
look at my smile
the pain you feel
is for just a short while

i can't wait to see you
and hope you do too
cuz you were meant
for me to love you

                                                                         continued ...

(he)

i get a feel
that you are the one
can it be
my dreams have come true?

love never lies
it always lives on
in my heart
from me to love you

(she)

no inhibitions
my soul is sweet
express your love
make my world complete

i feel our vibe baby
yes i do
you be for me
what i'll be for you

                                                continued ...

(he)

i've gotta learn
to love once more
am i afraid to fall again?

i have to be
and let me go
to hope this love never ends

(she)

my feelings for you
will never hide
so don't cover the hurt
or the love inside

follow your heart
let your dreams flow
i wanna be your sunshine
your morning glow

*continued ...*

(he)

i want to hear
your voice in every way
make it the first
and the last of each day

i want to feel your body
late at night
for then i will know
our vibe is right

(she)

you need to hear my voice
each and everyday
only then you'll see
love will be okay

our love will be true
let's hold each other tight
you've got to believe
that this love is right

continued ...

(he)

i guess i feel
what you've always known
this lonely king
needs his queen
by the throne

forever they say
when love is for real
i now understand
just how they feel

(she)

let's love each other
until we can't anymore
so when you fall
let it be
through love's door

you and i
will never ever end
just believe in us
and let your heart mend

continued ...

**refrain**

(together)

trust me baby
let's love all night
i think we got it
this vibe is right

you're my angel eyes
and i don't know why
but by loving you
my heart never dies

angel eyes
my angel eyes
want to be with you
until the end of time

angel eyes
my angel eyes
want to thank my maker
that you're in my life

# diversion

# your butt

**verse**

all over town
as i walk around
i see them all
packing downtown

some moving quickly
some standing still
some looking pretty
some looking ill

baby got back
she'll break your neck
baby walk by
hope my date forgets

some all muscle
some all fat
some just jiggle
some like that

i tried not looking
yet there it was
i got in trouble
just because

some all big
some all small
some just sag
there's a butt for all

**refrain**

i like your butt
it makes me smile

i like your butt
it runs a mile

i like your butt
it steals my eye

i like your butt
it's so damn fine

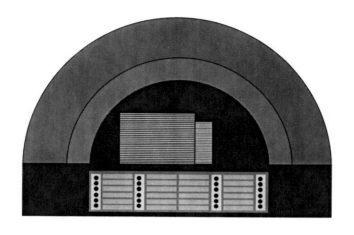

# inspired

# you gotta give

**verse**

you ever wonder why
you sit down and cry
you ever wonder why
your life just ain't right

you ever wonder why
your neighbor's got more
yet you haven't seen
behind their closed doors

it's a simple rule
about life you see
if you wanna have more
be more than just about "me"

you gotta learn
to give
you gotta
want to please
you gotta
give the thanks
get down on your knees

you ever wonder when
you gonna have it all
you ever lose your mind
to get up then fall

you gotta just believe
if you want it all
you gotta live your dreams
come on and stand tall

**refrain**

you gotta give
if you want to get back
it's a simple rule
love works like that

you gotta give
if you want it all
it's as simple
as walking tall

you gotta know
deep down inside
it's no mistake
why your alive

# just be true

**verse**

woke up this morning
with my feet on the ground
sun broke my window
felt the warmth all around

started to think
just how grateful i was
i got my own place
never broke any laws

got my coffee to go
and a job with a check
just a little rush hour
got my tunes on deck

i'm not going to worry
if i'm five minutes late
i'll be where i need to
cuz that's just my fate

i see all the madness
as i drive around
the homeless they wander
on all sides of town

the hustle and flow
business crowds in the street
i wonder how many
really chasing their dreams

continued ...

the news got me thinking
i gotta believe
that the world's not as good
as it was once conceived

the lies and the money
the greed the affairs
the people around me
living like they don't care

my family my love
maybe that's all i got
thank God they support me
sometimes life's not so hot

the moon now suspended
sits up in the sky
it gives me perspective
when i wonder why?


**refrain**

why
don't we help each other?
do we just run the other way
just be true to who you are
life
keep it simple everyday

just be true to who you are
just be true and you'll go far
just be true to let it be
above the horizon
there's more to see

# crazy dreams

**verse**

does it really matter?
when the sun goes up and down
does it really matter?
if your dreams are never found

crazy me for thinking
that maybe they would come true
crazy dreams inside my mind
i want to share with you

crazy as it seems
i'm believing they'll come true
in a hundred years from now
there's no more me or you

so chase that rainbow in the sky
live tomorrow yesterday
be your living crazy dreams
live them all the way

so wake up with the sun
let the soul of life be yours
let time belong to no one
and know there's always more

crazy maybe
i feel it in my soul
crazy maybe
life's in my control

crazy dreams
give hope to life each day
crazy dreams
like living your last day

## refrain

crazy dreams
crazy movies in my head
crazy dreams
loving life instead

crazy dreams
without you i'd be dead
crazy dreams just
keep living in my head

crazy dreams i'm thinking
can't be right
crazy dreams i know
this is my life

# just luck

**verse**

a broken clock
is right twice a day
once in a while
the fat man gets laid

a long putt
just sometimes goes in
once in a while
the faithful will sin

a blind squirrel
someday finds a nut
once in while
a wimp has some guts

a lost boat
one day will find shore
once in a while
your wife wants some more

a broke man
some day will eat steak
once in a while
the job gives you a break

about life
it's never so planned
things just so happen
try to understand

**refrain**

just give it a try
it's luck don't ask why
you'll just never know
it might be on your side

luck doesn't care
if you're ready or not
time keeps on moving
don't stare at the clock

got my lottery ticket
dreams big as can be
got nothing to lose
hoping maybe it's me

# laugh

### verse

laugh…
life is too hard
to frown through it all

laugh…
so what if you fall
just get up stand tall

laugh…
don't shed tears
just have a ball

laugh…
be nice
"karma's" a cycle after all

laugh…
believe in yourself
because there's no one else

laugh…
hate is just crazy
love makes things easy

laugh…
hell is on fire
heaven's my desire

**refrain**

don't forget to laugh
don't forget to dream

nothing in life
is ever what it seems

don't forget to live
don't forget to be

just believe in life
the simple things are free

# shake it off

**verse**

got the stress of your life
its weight on your shoulders
the monkey jumped on
so you know it ain't over

you try to hang on
and you try to pretend
got a smile on your face
even fooled all your friends

you cry in the dark
and pray to get better
got no one to talk to
in this stormy weather

you look for the rainbow
the promise once told
you follow its colors
there ain't no more gold

you toss all night long
insomnia your friend
you sleep in the sun
wonder when it will end

you believe in your dream
and know that it's true
no one can stop you
cause in faith you'll be new

**refrain**

shake it off
don't feel alone
Dave beat Goliath
with one little stone

shake it off
just do believe
Jesus did die
for you to receive

# ask

**verse**

just believe in yourself
the sun shines after rain

just believe for a moment
laughter follows our pain

just believe in yourself
cause no one else ever will

just believe in yourself
you're the king of your hill

just believe in yourself
things can only get better

just believe in yourself
you create your own weather

just believe in yourself
lift your eyes to the sky

just believe in Jesus
and you'll know why he died

ask to have all you want
believe it's yours and you'll see

that's what faith is about
have it all to receive

**refrain**

ask
believe and receive
that's the secret to life

ask
believe and receive
everything is alright

ask
believe and receive
the time is now right

# let "you" be

**verse**

from across the room
i see her
sitting there
bald like me
i thought my life had trouble
but she gets chemotherapy

thought i had it bad
it seemed
my troubles
now no more
every time i see her smile
can't wait to walk in her door

she couldn't breathe
but laughed away
forgot
that she was sick
i wiped my tears the other day
cuz her time will soon be quick

my lesson learned
is that in life
regret
won't get you far
just remember to accept in conflict
the person that you are

cherish those
close to you
hug them everyday
remember that in troubled times
pain will pass
cuz there's another day

**refrain**

let it go
it's not so bad
cuz what you hold
you never had

let it be
and you'll see
that one day
you'll be free

let it live
your soul alive
it ain't so bad
it'll be alright

let it love
your heart again
what you are
will never end

just let you be
just let you be
cuz just so soon
you're spirit's free

# live my dreams

**verse**

i came to say goodbye
and i don't know why
God chose so soon for you to go

because i now live
with dreams to chase
i'll never see your smile and glow

one of my best
one of few friends
we both stared cancer down

you leave behind
your only child
for you
chemo didn't turn things around

i learned to live
and just believe
God knows his reasons why

i guess there's more
more dreams to dream
a purpose for my life

i cannot judge
or fight the life
that God has planned for me

continued ...

i take my box
unwrap my cloth
of dreams that now live free

i now will live
with love and purpose
it's deep inside my soul

i'll never question
the reasons why
God chose to let you go


**refrain**

i take control
of my life now
with true divinity

i take a breath
to hear the love
that lives inside of me

# suspended

**verse**

i've been to the other side
and seen the light
i've felt at peace suspended
somehow i was alright

i've seen the horizon
beyond the mountain limit
i've felt no tears or pain
somehow reborn in spirit

i've seen my loved ones
i've broken bread and wine
i've felt no worries
somehow suspended in time

i've seen my father
an image of myself
i've always believed
after life there's something else

**refrain**

suspended
i left the world behind

suspended
there is no sense of time

suspended
i now feel so alive

suspended
it's like i never died

# **water**

### **verse**

let me be your water
let me soothe your soul

let me drown away your troubles
help you set your goals

let me guide your ship
let me take you to shore

let me put out your fires
so you regain control

let me show you now
all that i can do

let me show you water
that sees you through

let me be with you
whether it's cold or hot

faith is in your water
just trust in your heart

**refrain**

like water
let me quench your soul

like water
let me live in you

like water
i'll make u feel so good

like water i'll make you feel
brand new

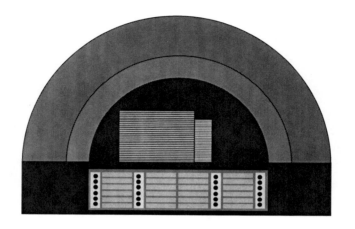

# diversion

# the designer

**verse**

wicked design
look at those lines
designed by a brother
ahead of his time

wicked talent
born raw they say
his visions are passion
he still draws all day

wicked cars
grills in your face
return a corporation
ahead of its pace

wicked rides
zero to fly
HEMI packed engines
SRTs in disguise

wicked
just wicked my man
he's movin ahead
watchout in Japan

**refrain**

a legend born
the man can draw

a hot designer
now drive your new car

a prodigy
never seen before

designs so timely
we want some more

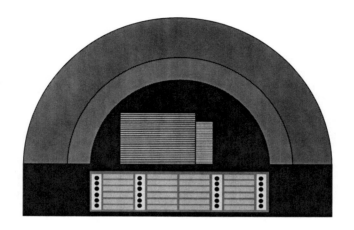

# turbulence

# missing you

**verse**

can't erase your messages
or empty the room
since you've been gone

can't concentrate
on the littlest of things
i feel so alone

can't believe i've lost my love
my best friend
to start again

can't believe you left
i grieve this loss
in shock, so sudden?

i can imagine you
in heaven
at peace without pain

i can imagine you
without fear
keeps me from going insane

**refrain**

i just imagine
you smiling above

i just imagine
you're feeling pure love

i just imagine
that one day we'll be

together again
just you and me

# did i turn you off ?

**verse**

it just started so good
we'd be talking all night
we didn't need a plan
cuz we never did fight

it just came to a bore
or things just went wrong
i felt you pull back
and sing a new song

was it something i said
or just didn't do
was it the way that i touched
making love to you

didn't i pull your chair
open up the door
compliment your dress
kiss you even more

did i turn you off ?
make you turn away
should i do something
to make you stay

was it the shoes i wore
or my jeans too tight
was it my cologne
that made you act not right

i guess i gotta go
since i just can't stay
you got me thinking
i just should go away

**refrain**

did i turn you off?
bore you on the phone
did my words offend
wish you left alone

did i turn you off?
make you love me less
i have no clue
this i must confess

did i turn you off?
cuz i can move on
i got my pride
if there's nothing wrong

did i turn you off?
just let me know
it ain't no thing
if you want it slow

# forgive me girl

**verse**

i'll sing you a love song
and make you love me back
i'll touch you in ways that show you
it's as simple as that

i'll rebuild my world
and make you my queen
i'll regain your trust
if you forgive what you've seen

i know that it's hard
to accept the hurt you feel
i promise to show you
help to love and to heal

i'd hate to give up
on these years of our lives
i've broken the promise
when i made you my wife

i understand really
if it is over for you
these are the chances we take
when we don't follow through

i'll pray that our love
makes us stronger this time
sometimes painful lessons
is the age in life's wine

i'll wait here to see
if my heart's been forgiven
i know i'm not perfect
but at least i've learned living

**refrain**

i know you might forgive me
i know you might move on
just remember i'm so sorry
for doing you so wrong

i know things turned nasty
i know they crushed your soul
just remember that i love you
even if you choose to go

forgive me
forgive me girl
just remember
that you're my world

forgive me
forgive me now
please love
and take me back somehow

# don't try

**verse**

don't walk through that door
i can't love u no more
i can't take the games you play
since you ain't gonna stay

don't come kissing me
don't wanna touch your lips
love shouldn't be this hard
i want your hand not fingertips

don't come huggin me
i can't squeeze u no more
can't take all the pretend
when we know it's the end

don't lie or try to call
you wouldn't catch me if i fall
there's nothing left to give
so don't even ask what if ?

don't ever just forget
i'm the best that you'll regret
your chance to have my love
disappeared when you gave up

**refrain**

don't try crawlin
if you ain't steppin

don't try beggin
if you ain't lovin

don't forget
to love yourself

cuz if you can't love me
there's no one else

# got a fake life

**verse**

got married yesterday
never felt right from the start
the longest final act
before it all just fell apart

the diamond never big enough
the house was just too small
the ride never too cool enough
no Mercedes after all

one job was never good enough
thought two was to maintain
the things we never really owned
just painfully sustained

the sex was never really there
the chemistry so stale
had both of us just living lies
in a marriage that had failed

the kids bring out the best in us
they keep the smiles alive
oblivious to reality
that something just ain't right

we gotta try hard
and let each other go
cuz where we end up
just nobody knows

continued ...

pressure from the family
they ain't behind the scenes
they think they have the answers
yet their lives
not so serene


**refrain**

i'm living a fake life
feeling nothing
trying to do right

i'm living a fake life
just knowing
that this can't be right

# separate lives

**verse**

it started good
between you and me
it seemed so right
we were family

i've grown to love you
without a doubt
but having us forever
it just won't work out

they say it's hard
to keep it alive
the magic once
that breathed in our lives

our friends keep calling
to keep us together
but never knew
our stormy weather

i just can't tell
if i'm wrong or right
but i can't go on
if all we do is fight

life is too short
for me to believe
to live like this
is hard to conceive

continued ...

i gotta move on
and start living again
we've grown apart
but i still love you as a friend

for now our lives
are taking different paths
we need a new beginning
there is no going back


**refrain**

separate lives
is what i'm feeling
separate lives
it's just our being

is it wrong
to want it all
is it wrong
to let love fall

# so be

**verse**

so be it
cuz i know how you feel
so obvious to me
what we got ain't real

i knew it
from your hug last night
it was so cold
it just wasn't right

you can't deny
that you miss me so
i can't believe
that you'd just let go

you miss me
remember you said
stop playing games
you're messing with my head

if you let me go
my love just can't stay
my heart's the balloon
that just floats away

i'll be over you
if you wait too long
my love for you
can't stay in this wrong

### refrain

so be
i gotta let go
i can't live your lie
it's hurting me so

so be
i gotta move on
i can't hurt like this
and live in the wrong

so be
so be it
love sometimes hurts
i'm calling it quits

so be
so be it
i'm letting you go
i'm just over it

# restless

### verse

caught in a dream
visions of you
i open my eyes
find me next to you

restless nights
i toss and i turn
these four walls
make me wish
you'd return

i promise to love you
touch your heart and your mind
i miss you more
than forever in time

don't try to leave
give me a chance
just let me show you
i am your man

**refrain**

i'm restless
just laying here

i'm restless
time's standing still

i'm restless
i want you bad

i'm restless
without you i'm sad

# suspicions

**verse**

i've got this intuition
that you've been out just creepin
i've got strange suspicions
that it's not me that your feelin

forgot to kiss goodbye again
i stopped to ask you why
your lunchbreak calls to check on me
have withered and just died

i wonder now what happens
why this love no longer works
did you ever truly love me ?
or were you always just a flirt ?

i've learned that love's a challenge
about your core and who you are
the most important lesson
is that you love yourself by far

in my heart i know my soul mate
will cross my path in time
this i must believe
so my soul will never die

**refrain**

suspicions
you've lost your love for me

suspicions
the truth now sets me free

suspicions
i won't give up and die

suspicions
there's a love for me in time

# gotta go

**verse**

i thought i knew
you from the start
your looks your walk
that stole my heart

the little smile
that caught my eyes
a presence
that just mesmerized

come to find
your not so true
the little lies
caught up to you

you had me fooled
i can't believe
i didn't see
what you conceived

i need to go
i hope you find
the truly wrong
that's in your mind

i hope you'll get the help
you need
i'm letting go
this just can't be

## refrain

gotta go
this ain't for me

gotta go
to what i need

gotta go
no mystery

gotta go
i'm flyin free

# over you

**verse**

hello my Monday
my rainbow in the sky
hello my sunrise
it's gonna be alright

my past few days
thought my storm would never end
couldn't concentrate
because i lost a best friend

got a fresh start
follow my heart again
heartache ain't easy
i smile to just pretend

it's gonna be alright
i won't breakdown or cry
i'll get over you
and no longer ask why

you made me stronger
better than i was
in faith no worries
at peace just because

if our paths cross
i thought i'd let you know
my heartbreak's over
i've already let go

**refrain**

i know the sun will shine
my storm will pass in time

i just keep moving on
live my life toward the sun

# goodbye my love

**verse**

guess
it's gone
what we had
is done

the love we once
shared
is no longer
one

the laughter
and joy
when love
was real

replaced by
sadness and the pain
we
feel

to have what once was good
to live
it all again

the risk would be too great
i'd rather
just be friends

                                                        continued ...

although
i have forgiven
the hurt
you put on me

the love
i have inside
is strong
so now i'm free

the choice
i've made
is true
i have no more regrets

i wish
you all the love
and nothing
but the best


**refrain**

goodbye my love
my love

goodbye my friend
my friend

lessons we learn
we learn

hello to life
again

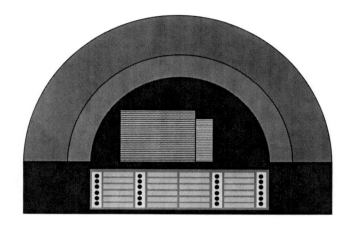

# diversion

# sticky wicky

**verse**

i'm moving in
i see you dancin
you lookin good
champagne is pourin

we celebrate
steppin is feelin
you glide across
my soul is healin

are u alone ?
i see your girlfriends
they laughin hard
but i got your hand

give me the time
can't wait to show you
these lips are good
and workin for you

you gotta give me
some sticky kissy
i'll let you have
my sticky wicky

don't play the game
if you ain't dealin
i'm here to play
no heart for stealin

**refrain**

sticky kissy
can't get enough

sticky wicky
let me show you love

sticky kissy
come dance with me

sticky wicky
laugh and let it be

sticky
sticky
wicky
wicky

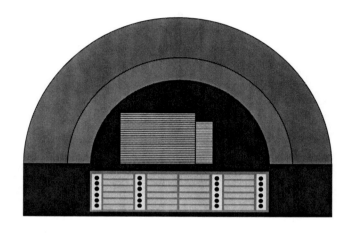

# perspective

# troubled

**verse**

troubled i remain
another day is done
reflections conversation
with my maker we are one

my troubled tired spirit
seeks comfort from the soul
my life is just too much
maybe i should just let go

victimized i wonder
when these pains will pass
a restless mind i'm sleepless
how long can this last ?

save me, hold my hand
cuz i feel like letting go
the pain it lives inside
i just can't take no more

i pray for guidance
kneeling everyday
hope the hurt to rise
and simply go away

i'm falling back believing
and hope that you will be
the promise in my life
to my serenity

you promised to protect me
that i would no longer fall
i saw you die for me
a cross the burden of it all

**refrain**

are you troubled ?
troubled about your life
are you troubled ?
cuz things are never right

don't give up
have faith in me
hold my hand
for my love
will set you free

# gotta move on

**verse**

woke up in my bed
dreams of yesterday
crowd my mind in every way

got to thinking
how lucky i was
standing here just today

working last night
saw a family lose
a loved one again

teenage girl
family trip
another semester ends

head on hit
drunkard lives
only dad survives

gotta tell him
only he lives
and i don't know why

an e.r. doc
i see it all
and i just don't understand

trauma takes
you by surprise
enemies and friends

continued ...

tears run dry
gotta be strong
another day now awaits

i wish i could
just hold your hand
but i gotta have faith

today's pain
untimely blows
gotta stand and be strong

just some things
i'll never get
like the right from the wrong

it's not for me
to judge or feel
only wish for the best

the people i see
the faces i help
i try to give them rest


**refrain**

gotta live
nothing's promised
you just don't know

gotta love
give your thanks
no regrets when you go

# butterfly rage

**verse**

butterfly still
caught in my grill
road rage late
just can't take a break

so used to moving
just thinking fast
i'm in a hurry
can't get there last

cell phones busy
can't talk right now
roads are raging
get to work somehow

it never mattered
now that i've chilled
all that rushing
and time stood still

running red lights
and cruzin stops
all that changed
my mood is now hot

gotta slow down
let a butterfly float
love those colors
back on the road

gonna get movin
without all the stress
i ain't worried
gonna get there yet

**refrain**

got a butterfly
caught in my grill

colors beautiful
time stands still

gotta slow down
before i die

the stress in life
makes me want to fly

# paycheck

**verse**

a cold winter night
steam rises a manhole
lays a man
an unknown soul

a home of bundled
shredded cardboard sheets
tears trickling
shivers frostbitten feet

a cup stands empty
right by his side
shaken and rattled
a penny shattered pride

i walk to him
i feel an obligation
can i change a life ?
with my small donation

i often wonder
what brings a man down
land of opportunity
and look what i found

i stand no better
than this man on his knees
one paycheck from nothing
and a wallet empty

i pray one day
that we'll all be free
have supper together
with dignity

**refrain**

one paycheck from nothing
could be you and me

one paycheck eviction
don't start feeling free

one paycheck my spirit
i give what i can

one paycheck that's life
i don't understand

# my 911

**verse**

got my 911
my love my passion
12 years of med school
got my education

i'm a hard working brother
on the way to work
i was born to save lives
i was blessed at birth

got another brother down
another bad call
the guns in these streets
now a brother must fall

another late night
i'm burning all lights
gotta get to work
if i'm gonna save this life

got a nice looking ride
it was born to fly
a design by my brother
a perfection to eyes

gotta save this life
driving my last mile
sirens in my mirror
cuz i've been profiled

continued ...

got another trauma red
my scrubs bloodshed
gotta tell another mother
her baby boy is dead

gotta break it to the family
i did the best i could
young brothers just like me
whose lives can still be good

gotta be a role model
to these young men
need more of us
so they will understand

**refrain**

got my 911
got a powerful mind

got my 911
not a powerful gun

# patriot

**verse**

i wake up in my bed
got my coffee in my hand
read the paper
and it's war
and i just don't understand

got my soldier
fighting hard
for me to go to work
overseas with little hope
he missed his daughter's birth

Starbucks
cappuccino
Beemers valet park
i-pod pleasure music
my soldier sleeps in the dark

rush hour
stressed at work
the wife the kids at play
come home to hugs to feel the love
a soldier's family
peace evades

steak
movies dinner
not worried about my bills
golfing with my buddies
my soldier's best friend killed

continued ...

sleep
much needed
in my king size bed
rested i awaken
my soldier is now dead


**refrain**

missiles shot
grenades rock
soldiers in the trenches
fighting hard
enemy lines
this war hasn't ended

patriot
you my patriot
respect for you lives here
i have my life
i have my wife
because you have no fear

patriot
you my patriot
stay strong we love you so
i know it's hard
hang in there and don't ever let go

# tin shed

**verse**

above the clouds
a scenic country
first black republic
welcome to Haiti

in history
so little people know
Toussaint was a slave
defeated all his foes

not long ago
1804 to be exact
rebels fought hard
got their country back

liberated free
never done before
a slave revolution
but now a country poor

dictators
bled the country down
now i see the truth
on solid ground

poverty illiteracy
all around
Macoute got people
running into ground

continued ...

babies busting famine
bellies all about
tin sheds standing hollow
on a ground in drought

what can i do
to help relieve the pain
HIV got the country
so tragically insane

educate America
just recognize
a Haitian founded chi-town
and won a civil war prize


**refrain**

tin shed
a poor boy starves again

tin shed
America eats out again

tin shed
u probably sleep in bed

tin shed
when you wake this boy is dead

# look for love

**verse**

let the dove
fly up on high
let the love lessons
never die

so many of
the young leave
the reasons
why we grieve

the violence in the world
hopeless
no end to it all
addicted to the drugs
is why we all will fall

executives now stealing
politicians dealing drugs
prostitutes now mothers
with deadbeat daddy thugs

money greed and power
a formula to the end
families now stay broken
depression just sets in

you think you had it made
past decisions now regrets
your driving second hand
your neighbor's in a Vette

continued ...

you give up on your dreams
the house you got now stale
reminds you of your past
your neighbor's now in jail

you had a simple life
as a kid without a gun
life did not contaminate
all you had was fun

now you risk to lose it all
devil works your every move
gotta be strong and resist
intuition has the clue

just believe that life is short
a journey with no end
avoid the contradictions
let your heart bring misery's end

**refrain**

be strong
don't let go
believe in yourself
you can always have more

nothing lasts forever
except in your dreams
nothing is as bad
as what it seems

illusions deceptions look around
somewhere in the turmoil
love can be found

look for love
feel the love

look for love
if you had enough

# forgive

**verse**

look at yourself
before you criticize another
look at yourself
at the wood in your own eye

look at yourself
before you spread another rumor
look at yourself
before you tell another lie

look at yourself
do you think you're the greatest
look at yourself
the mirror of insecurity

look at yourself
it's time to look inside
look at yourself
it's time to face reality

learn to forgive
accept all imperfection
learn to forgive
change your hearts' direction

**refrain**

forgive
forgive, that's the simple truth

forgive
forgive, someone died for you

forgive
forgive, now the past is gone

forgive
forgive, you must just move on

# perspective

**verse**

watch u got
can be taken away
in just a split second
any day

don't take for granted
what you have in time
get inpatient
you're in back of the line

put in perspective
what you really see
realize first
you're just blessed to be

all of your abilities
blessed in disguise
appreciate this
the fact you're alive

stay strong
and you'll realize
that life is hard
you're not paralyzed

believe with your mind
your heart knows the truth
faith through the grind
and you'll see a new you

it doesn't matter
if you try and fall
just believe in the maker
and you'll rise above all

**refrain**

paralyzed
in a hospital bed

all that he sees
is the ceiling ahead

lonely
cuz he can't share his thoughts

tears just run dry
cuz his visits have dropped

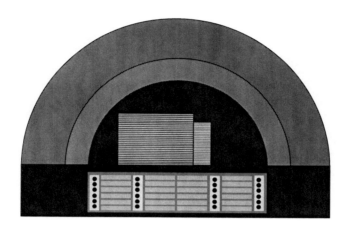

# diversion

# Vegas girl

**verse**

Vegas in my blood
can't get enough
running the strip
don't know which way's up

Vegas and friends
we're single again
girls got me drinking
martinis and gin

Vegas in stitches
got me laughing so hard
forgot my shoes
at the piano bar

Vegas got me singing
karaoke style
give me a drink
and i'll sing all wild

Vegas going crazy
pain in my wallet
chips i just keep losing
there's a hole in my pocket

Vegas and the girls
can't retire tonight
gotta look good
might meet mr. right

Vegas lost time
i've been up with the moon
gotta get a nap
sunrise is soon

**refrain**

got Vegas in my blood
a chill in my bones
what happened in Vegas
gotta leave it alone

catch a redeye flight
gotta leave it behind
what happened in Vegas
never happened in time

# about the author

"67 lyrics 4 u" is the second published work from author Maxime Alix Gilles. His first book, "Scriptures of Life: A Collection of Poems", was published in 1998.

An emergency room physician for more than a decade, Maxime's lyrics expand on some of the themes in his first book, i.e., the different facets of love and relationships. His window on the intimate thoughts and feelings of others fuels his writing. It is indicative of his desire to reach out to musicians and readers in a way that differs from his day-to-day professional milieu. In a screenplay, Maxime's life experience would effectively cast him in the roles of reporter and actor.

Maxime is a proud Haitian-American and the father of three happy and healthy children. He practices medicine in a suburb of Chicago.

Gary Hannabarger Studios
@ *www.hannabargerphoto.com*

Printed in the United States
206858BV00002B/159/P